URBAN LEGEND

Written By Christopher Harris

For Publishing Information, contact Journal Joy:
Info@thejournaljoy.com.
www.thejournaljoy.com

Paperback ISBN: 978-1-957751-61-0
Ebook ISBN: 978-1-957751-63-4
Editor: Nicole Gyimah

First Paperback edition, 2023

This book is dedicated to my son, Christopher Harris Jr.

This book is the beginning of a long process of learning about life for him. The influences he may encounter growing up, and the choices he will have to make will be what impacts his life.

My son: just know the choices you make will be very important and know you always have support!

Urban child what will your legend be?

ENGINEER

RAP

DOCTOR

SCIENTIST

He woke up ready for his day to start.
Time to get ready to set himself apart.

He came from a place where no father figure was present.
He came from a place where being a man meant learning from your own lessons.

He thought to himself, was school really best?
He usually hangs with guys who know the streets.
Maybe I should hang with the rest.

There's so much around him, that he doesn't know what to do.
Social media influencers, rappers, and athletes living the good life: yeah he wants that luxury too.

Having a mind of your own may be his best bet.
Making a name for himself so that his family will be set.

But back to the people he knows best,
the guys in the streets who put him to the test.

Should I join them and have to ask myself this same question

The decisions you make will have a huge impact, whether it's being an athlete or being musically talented.

You may choose to build a career as a video game developer and create the next Fortnite.
What you decide will come from the heart, making those around you happy.

You choose what makes you rise to the top!

The legend this kid makes will be his choice to make!

About the Author:

My name is Christopher Harris. I am currently a teacher leader working in metro Atlanta. I currently hold two Master's degrees in Education and in Business Administration.

I have been working with youth for about 8 years and have been trying to make an impact on the lives of everyone I encounter. I strive to do more with the knowledge that I have obtained in order to encourage my son to achieve whatever his heart desires.

www.ingramcontent.com/pod-product-compliance
Lightning Source LLC
Chambersburg PA
CBHW041450120626
46547CB00002B/405